Machines at Work

Machines at the Airport

Siân Smith

Raintree

Raintree is an imprint of Capstone Global Library Limited, a company incorporated in England and Wales having its registered office at 7 Pilgrim Street, London, EC4V 6LB – Registered company number: 6695582

www.raintreepublishers.co.uk
myorders@raintreepublishers.co.uk

Text © Capstone Global Library Limited 2014
First published in hardback in 2014
Paperback edition first published in 2015
The moral rights of the proprietor have been asserted.

Edited by Dan Nunn and John-Paul Wilkins
Designed by Cynthia Akiyoshi
Picture research by Elizabeth Alexander
Production by Helen McCreath
Originated by Capstone Global Library Ltd
Printed and bound in Great Britain by
Ashford Colour Press Ltd, Gosport, Hampshire

ISBN 978 1 406 25936 0 (hardback)
17 16 15 14 13
10 9 8 7 6 5 4 3 2 1

ISBN 978 1 406 25941 4 (paperback)
18 17 16 15 14
10 9 8 7 6 5 4 3 2 1

British Library Cataloguing in Publication Data
Smith, Siân.
Machines at the airport. – (Machines at work)
387.7'36'0284-dc23
A full catalogue record for this book is available from the British Library.

Acknowledgements
We would like to thank the following for permission to reproduce photographs: Alamy pp. 4 (© Steve Vidler), 5 (© ITAR-TASS Photo Agency), 9 (© Kevpix), 12 (© ROUSSEL BERNARD), 15 (© Tips Images / Tips Italia Srl a socio unico), 18 (© imagebroker), 19 (© Richard Wareham Fotografie), 22 (© Jim West); BULMOR Airground Technologies GmbH p. 13; Corbis pp. 7 (© Angelika Warmuth/dpa), 17 (© Patrice Latron); Getty Images pp. 6, 8 (Baerbel Schmidt/Stone+), 10, 23 conveyor belt (Erik Dreyer/Stone); Shutterstock pp. 14, title page (© Robert Cumming), 16, 23 tug (© Thomas Nord), 21, 23 pilot (© Andresr), 23 scanner (© Voznikevich Konstantin), 23 fuel (© Concept Photo), 23 X-ray (© Kasza), 23 radar (© Gertan), SuperStock pp. 11 (© imagebroker.net), 20 (© Ton Koene / age footstock).

Design element photographs of aeroplane (© oriontrail), airport runway (© Cindy Hughes), car engine part (© fuyu liu), and gear cog (© Leremy) reproduced with permission of Shutterstock.

Front cover photograph of an aeroplane reproduced with permission of Getty Images (Yuji Kotani/Taxi Japan). Back cover photograph of an air traffic controller holding light wands (© Andresr) and a tug (© Thomas Nord) reproduced with permission of Shutterstock.

Every effort has been made to contact copyright holders of material reproduced in this book. Any omissions will be rectified in subsequent printings if notice is given to the publisher.

Contents

Some words are shown in bold, **like this**. You can find out what they mean by looking in the glossary.

Why do we have machines at an airport?

People make machines to do different jobs.

An aeroplane is a machine that helps us to travel to places that are far away.

People go to airports so that they can travel on aeroplanes.

Some machines at airports help people to get their bags onto aeroplanes.

Can a machine spot dangerous things?

People are not allowed to take things onto aeroplanes that could hurt other people.

Metal detectors are machines that can tell if people are carrying guns, knives, or other metal objects.

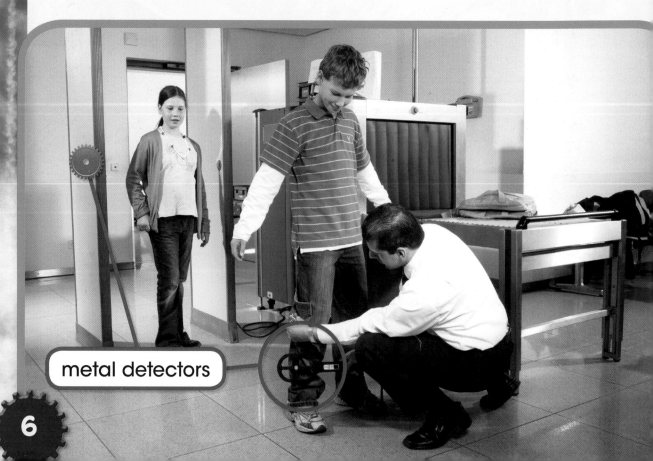

metal detectors

Some machines can take pictures of people that look a bit like an **X-ray**.

They can show if people have hidden things under their clothes.

Every bag at an airport has to go through an **X-ray** machine.

X-ray machines show pictures of things inside a bag, even when it is closed.

X-ray machine

Different colours show what things are made of.

Airport workers check to see if the pictures show anything dangerous.

How can machines help to move bags?

Each bag is given a number. Computers and **scanners** use the number to tell where each bag is and where it needs to go.

Moving belts called **conveyor belts** and carts carry the bags around.

conveyor belt

conveyor belt

belt loader

Sorting machines stop the bags from getting lost or stuck.

Special machines called belt loaders move bags onto the aeroplanes.

How can machines help to move people?

The doors on an aeroplane are high above the ground.

A giant staircase on wheels helps people to get on and off an aeroplane.

ambulift

If people cannot walk, small buggies can help them to move around an airport.

A machine called an ambulift can lift them up into an aeroplane.

What are the biggest machines at an airport?

The biggest machines at an airport are the aeroplanes.

Jet aeroplanes can carry hundreds of people.

Inside an aeroplane, there are many small machines that help the **pilot**.

Machines show the pilot how fast the plane is going, where the plane is, and how high it is in the air.

What other machines help aeroplanes?

Aeroplanes use their engines to move forward, but most cannot go backwards.

An aeroplane tractor or **tug** moves an aeroplane to where it needs to be.

tug

refueller truck

hose

Aeroplanes are too big to go to petrol stations, but they need **fuel** to make them move.

Refueller trucks with long hoses give aeroplanes the fuel they need.

Which machines help aeroplanes in the ice and snow?

Aeroplanes need to go fast down a runway before they can take off into the air.

Snow ploughs push snow off runways so that planes can take off.

snow plough

runway

de-icer machine

Some parts of an aeroplane stop working if they are covered in ice.

De-icer machines lift airport workers up so they can spray special liquid to melt the ice.

What stops aeroplanes crashing into each other?

Airport workers guide planes around airports, so that they do not crash into each other.

Pictures from **radars** show them any planes in the sky and where they are going.

radar picture

light wand

Airport workers tell **pilots** when it is safe to land by using radios.

They also use light wands to tell pilots what to do when they are on the ground.

What does this machine do?

Can you guess what this airport machine does?

Find the answer on page 24.

Picture glossary

 **conveyor belt** moving belt that carries things along

 **scanner** machine that reads information from a label

 **fuel** liquid we put into aeroplanes to make them move

 **tug** type of tractor that pulls things along

 **pilot** driver of an aeroplane

 **X-ray** photo that shows the inside of something

 **radar** machine that can tell where aeroplanes are in the sky and which direction they are moving in

Find out more

Books

A Day at the Airport (Time Goes By), Sarah Harrison (Millbrook Press, 2009)

Working at the Airport (21st Century Junior Library: Careers), Katie Marsico (Cherry Lake Pub., 2009)

Website

www.funkidslive.com/features/the-airport
Find out all about airports.

Index

The airport machine on page 22 is a water truck. It collects waste from the toilets of the aeroplane.